TONY EVANS
SPEAKS OUT ON
HEAVEN
AND HELL

TONY EVANS
SPEAKS OUT ON
HEAVEN AND HELL

MOODY PRESS
CHICAGO

Scripture quotations are taken from the *New American Standard Bible*®, ©
Copyright The Lockman Foundation 1960, 1962, 1963, 1968, 1971,
1972, 1973, 1975, 1977, 1995. Used by permission.

ISBN: 0-8024-4367-2

1 3 5 7 9 10 8 6 4 2

Printed in the United States of America

HEAVEN AND HELL

THE REALITY OF DEATH

L et me give you a fact that shouldn't surprise you. Unless Jesus Christ returns in our lifetime, we are all going to die.

You may be saying, "I know that, Tony. What's your point?" My point is that many people are trying to deny or dodge the truth of that simple fact, even though their eternal destiny is at stake. Our culture tries to camouflage death, dress it up, use soothing terms like "pass away" and "laid to rest" to talk about it. But the reality is that you and I are marching toward a date with death.

My purpose in this booklet is to bring us face-to-face with that reality, and to answer the question of what awaits us beyond the grave by examining what God's Word says about heaven and hell. Everybody has an opinion, from the atheist who says there's nothing beyond death to the universalist who says God is waiting with open arms to receive all of His creatures.

But anybody other than Jesus Christ who gives you an opinion about death, heaven, and hell is giving you an uninformed opinion. So don't let anybody who hasn't been there tell you about eternity, because you can't afford to get this one wrong. Let's set the stage for our discussion of heaven and hell with several important facts about the reality of death.

Death Is an Appointment

The first thing we need to know about death is that it is not a random event. The Bible says, "It is appointed for men to die once and after this comes judgment" (Hebrews 9:27). Every person who has ever lived will die by appointment. People may be late for a lot of events on earth, but this is one appointment everyone will be on time for, because it has been set by God.

The story is told of a man who came face-to-face with death one day. The man was standing on a street corner in his city when a stranger walked by. The stranger looked at the man in surprise, but said nothing and kept on walking.

When the man learned that the stranger was Death, he became afraid and went to a wise friend for advice. "Death just walked by and looked surprised to see me. What should I do?"

The wise friend said, "If I were you, I'd flee to another city far away."

So the man got ready and that night fled to a far-away city. But as he was walking on the streets of that city the next day, he was horrified to run into Death. "I thought I left you behind in my home city yesterday," the terrified man said to Death.

Death replied, "That's why I was so surprised to see you there yesterday. I have an appointment to meet you here today." All of us have a God-ordained appointment with death we will most definitely meet when the time comes.

Death Is a Conjunction

The common idea of death as the end of human existence is not what the Bible means when it talks about death. In the Bible, death involves *separation,* never cessation.

Most people think we are in the land of the living on our way to the land of the dying. But actually, we are in the land of the dying on our way to the land of the living. That's why I say death is a conjunction, not a period. It is the bridge between this life and the life to come.

We'll see that later in a familiar passage from the Word of God, Jesus' teaching in Luke 16. In this story of the rich man and Lazarus, Jesus said, "The poor man died *and,*" then "the rich man also died *and*" (v. 22, italics added). Luke 16 could have been a very short chapter if Jesus had simply said, "These men died, period." That would have been the end of the story.

But the Bible knows nothing of a concept of death that means the person ceases to exist. Death is the separation of our temporary, material body from the eternal, immaterial part of our being, the spirit or soul. James 2:26 says, "The body without the spirit is dead," but the opposite is not true. Our souls were created to live forever.

The Bible says our bodies are dead without their immaterial part because the soul is what gives life to, or animates, the body. At his creation, Adam was just a shell made out of dust until God "breathed into his nostrils the breath of life; and [Adam] became a living being" (Genesis 2:7).

Adam had no personhood or life until he received his soul. You are who you are because of your soul, not your body. Your ultimate value is not in your body, but in your soul because it is the part of you that will live forever. When you die life is not over because the only part of you that died is your body. Some people say that at death, the soul sleeps until it is resurrected. But that view does not have any support in Scripture.

Paul's preference was "to be absent from the body and to be at home with the Lord" (2 Corinthians 5:8). He told the Philippians, "I am hard-pressed from both directions, having the desire to depart and be with Christ, for that is very much better" (1:23). It doesn't sound like he expected to go into a deep sleep in an unconscious state until the resurrection!

The Bible is clear that at the moment of death, our souls pass immediately into conscious existence in eternity, either in heaven or in hell. A lot of people think there's some kind of second chance after death.

God's Word says nothing about an intermediate state of purgatory after death in which we have a second chance to get our act together, have our sins dealt with over a period of time, and finally make it to heaven.

Others want to believe that at death, *every* person encounters a wonderful, warm light and a welcoming, forgiving Being, ready to escort the deceased person to paradise. But that's not what the Word says either.

Since death means immediate passage into the next life, the fact is that when they bring your body to the church for your funeral, you won't be there. A funeral, a burial, and a gravestone may give the look of finality to a person's life, but that's only the way it appears from the standpoint of earth.

The world puts a period after death, but from God's standpoint death is only a pause so brief it's not even worth trying to measure. Paul says that at the resurrection our bodies shall be changed "in the twinkling of an eye" (1 Corinthians 15:52).

That's how fast you and I will be in eternity when we die. Death is a conjunction, followed by a destination.

Death Is Followed by a Destination

In Luke 16:19–31, Jesus gave us a detailed picture of what happens when we die by peeling back the corner of eternity and giving us a glimpse into heaven and hell.

We'll deal with this foundational passage later on, so all I want to point out here is that both Lazarus and the rich man ended up somewhere when they died. The difference was in their destinations—the difference between eternal joy in heaven for Lazarus and eternal suffering in hell for the rich man.

A dying man once gathered his four children around him. To each of the first three he simply said, "Good night." But then he turned to his fourth child and said, "Good-bye, Son."

The young man said, "Dad, you told the others good night. Why did you tell me good-bye?"

The dying man answered, "Because they are Christians, and I'll see them in the morning in heaven. But you have not come to Christ, and unless you do I'll never see you again."

Taking the Sting Out of Death

What will happen when you die? That depends on what you have done with Jesus.

We can't afford to gamble on eternity.

If you know Him as Savior, you don't have to wake up in the middle of the night wondering what will happen to you when you die. Death won't sting you at all, because "the sting of death is sin" (1 Corinthians 15:56).

One day a little boy was riding in the car with his father when a bee flew in through the window and started buzzing around. The boy began to scream, "The bee is going to sting me!" But his father reached out and grabbed the bee. He held it in his hand for a few seconds, then released it.

The bee began to buzz around and the boy started to cry again. But his father said, "Son, you don't have to be afraid. All the bee can do now is make noise." Then Dad held out his hand, and there in the palm of his hand was the bee's stinger.

On the cross of Calvary, Jesus Christ took the stinger of sin, which is death. So all death can do now is make noise for those whose trust is in Jesus Christ.

Forever is too long to miss Christ. Eternity is a long time to suffer torment and the pain of regret. For Christians, this life is the only hell they will ever know. But for non-Christians, this life is the only heaven they will ever know.

Life is not a game. We can't afford to gamble on eternity. As we look first at what the Bible says about hell, and then about heaven, make sure you remove any doubt about where you will spend eternity.

WHAT IS HELL LIKE?

Thinking seriously and biblically about hell is not something most people do. But Christians need to understand what God has saved them from, and unbelievers need to be warned of the eternal judgment that awaits them unless they repent of their sins and turn to Christ for salvation.

I know it's not popular to talk about hell. It's not surprising that in one survey, 76 percent of the people polled believed in heaven, while only 6 percent believed in hell. But my goal is to be biblical, not popular.

A lot of people cope with the idea of hell by denying its reality. Some would argue that hell is a leftover superstition from the Dark Ages and that we are too enlightened in the twenty-first century to believe in such a medieval concept.

There are two other popular "coping mechanisms" that some people use to get around the Bible's clear teaching on hell. One is called annihilation, which teaches that unbelievers are not punished eternally after death, but are annihilated so that they simply cease to exist.

Another belief that avoids having to deal with hell is the teaching of universalism. There are different forms of this, but the basic idea is that because God is good and loving He wouldn't condemn anyone to a place of eternal torment. So in the end everybody will be saved, even non-Christians, because all roads eventually lead to God and to heaven.

This issue is so important that we must allow God to speak for Himself through His Word. We must subject our concepts of hell to God's revelation. So let's see what the Bible says about what hell is really like.

The Reality of Hell

The first fact we need to establish is the undeniable reality of hell. Let's start with a definition. Hell is the place of eternal exile where the ungodly will experience God's righteous retribution against sin forever. We are going to see that of all the suffering in hell, the worst is the fact that the lost are banished from God's presence forever.

Jesus believed hell was a real place, and He taught its reality throughout His ministry. While teaching on the judgment awaiting the Gentiles, Jesus called hell "eternal fire" and "eternal punishment" (Matthew 25:41, 46).

These are just two of many verses in which the Bible clearly teaches the reality of hell as a place of punishment. Jesus said more about hell than He did about either heaven or love. So if the Lord's teaching on hell isn't trustworthy, if He was deceiving us on the reality of this place, how do we know we can trust Him when He tells us about heaven?

This is the problem with those who try to pull out of the Bible only the parts they like, while denying the less pleasant parts. We can see the impossibility of this when we read the full text of Matthew 25:46. Jesus said concerning the unrighteous Gentiles being judged, "These will go away into eternal punishment, but the righteous into eternal life."

The word for "eternal" is the same in both instances, which means Jesus was teaching that hell is just as eternal, and as real, as heaven. Jesus also characterized hell as a place of never-ending punishment, a clear message that we can't skip, ignore, or water down.

Jesus also taught in the most stark terms that hell is a place to be avoided at all costs. He said in Matthew

18:8–9 it would be better for us to cut off a hand or a foot, or put out an eye, than to be condemned to hell.

Jesus wasn't teaching self-mutilation as a means of dealing with sin, because you can pluck out your eye and still be a lustful or envious person. He was telling us to do whatever it takes, no matter how radical, to rid our lives of sin, because sin can lead us into hell. It is better to lose some things in this life than to be lost for eternity in hell.

Another reason I know hell is real is that death is real. Death only exists because of sin. If there were no sin, there would be no death. The presence of physical death is a testimony to us of the unseen, eternal reality of what the Bible calls the "second death" (Revelation 20:14), or hell. Trying to deny hell is as futile as trying to deny death. Hell is a reality that won't go away just because people don't want to think about it.

The Residents of Hell

Who are the residents of hell?

Jesus made perhaps the most important statement in this regard when He said the unrighteous Gentile nations will hear this pronouncement of judgment: "Depart from Me, accursed ones, into the eternal fire which has been prepared for the devil and his angels" (Matthew 25:41).

Hell was not created for human beings, but as a place of eternal punishment for Satan and the fallen angels who joined him in his rebellion against God in heaven. Satan made five "I will" statements in his attempt to usurp the throne of God (Isaiah 14:12–14).

But Satan and his angels, who became the demons, failed in their rebellion. So God prepared a place to eternally remind them of the consequences of spiritual rebellion.

Satan chose to set himself in opposition to God. The fundamental fact about hell is that going there is a choice, a decision. There will be no resident in hell, demonic or human, who did not opt for spiritual rebellion against God.

Although God did not create hell for people, those who make the same choice Satan made will suffer the same judgment. Just as we have to choose Christ and heaven, unrepentant sinners will go to hell by choice, not by chance.

I can hear someone saying, "I don't know anybody who would deliberately choose to go to hell." It's true that if you asked people point-blank, "Do you want to spend eternity in a lake of fire?" most would quickly say no.

But the decision isn't that simple. You see, hell is the built-in consequence of rejecting Christ. Human beings in their natural state are already alienated from God and under His wrath. They make their choice when they refuse to repent and receive Christ's forgiveness for sin. All a sinner has to do to choose hell is to say to Jesus Christ, "I don't want You."

Someone has said that hell is the answer to the sinner's prayer. Jesus taught us to pray to God, "Thy will be done." But a rebellious sinner says to God, "*My* will be done." And God grants that person's request.

The problem is that a lot of the same people who say they don't want to spend eternity in hell would deny that they are wicked, rebellious sinners in need of God's forgiveness. Many people think they are on God's side, when all they really want is to ignore God, enjoy the goodies He provides, and then slide into a corner of heaven at the end.

But God doesn't play that game. Anyone who chooses to reject Him forfeits His benefits and incurs His wrath. If you don't want God, you don't get His heaven.

The existence of hell may be hard for some people to understand, but hell confirms the fact that we are uniquely significant to God.

Humans are the only creation made in God's image. That's why we have the capacity to make eternally significant choices. Plants and animals don't have this capacity because they don't bear God's image and, therefore, they aren't eternal creatures.

So the existence of hell is a testimony of our importance before God and the importance of our choices. In fact, even though unbelievers don't like to think of hell in terms of their own accountability to God, they usually don't have any problem agreeing that some people should pay for their sins.

Think of the tyrants and dictators of history who have caused the deaths of millions of people. Think of mass murderers, child molesters, rapists, and others who have taken evil to its very depths. When a criminal commits an especially heinous crime and comes up for trial, it's common to hear people say things like, "If there isn't a hell, there ought to be for a person like this."

It's interesting that even non-Christians agree certain people's sins are so bad they deserve to suffer forever for what they did. Human justice is relative, but God's justice is absolute, and He takes our choices very seriously because people are very important in His sight.

So let's affirm again what the Bible teaches. People go to hell because they choose to reject God and hold on to their sin, not because He just decides to send them there.

The Reason for Hell

When Jesus said in Matthew 25:41 that hell was prepared for the devil and his angels, He pointed to the reason God created this place of punishment.

We need to understand this or we miss the message of Scripture concerning God's attitude toward sin and the reason He has to punish it with eternal retribution.

We defined hell earlier as the place of eternal exile where the ungodly forever experience God's righteous retribution against sin. Hell is the expression of God's settled, eternal, unchanging wrath against sin (Revelation 21:8; 22:15).

This is important because God doesn't just fly into a rage when somebody does something that ticks Him

17

off. The Bible says God is "a righteous judge . . . who has indignation every day" (Psalm 7:11). God doesn't throw temper tantrums. His anger against sin is built into His nature.

Don't misunderstand, though. God's displeasure can reach a boiling point when sin reaches an intolerable level. Ask Sodom and Gomorrah what happens when God has His fill of sin.

Paul wrote in Romans 1:18, "The wrath of God is revealed from heaven against all ungodliness and unrighteousness of men who suppress the truth in unrighteousness."

At the core of this issue of hell is the righteous character of God. Later in Romans, after describing God's dealings with Israel, Paul said, "Behold then the kindness and severity of God" (11:22). God is both merciful and righteous. He is love, but He is also holy—so holy that He cannot even look at evil (Habakkuk 1:13). He must respond to sin.

If you saw a roach run across your kitchen counter, I doubt if you would just walk away and say, "Oh well, it's not bothering anybody." You are going to squash that bug because your nature doesn't allow you to tolerate insects in your kitchen.

God always responds to evil, in one of two basic ways. We might call them His passive and His active wrath.

Romans 1 is a good example of passive wrath because when people persisted in sin, God "gave them over" to follow their evil desires (vv. 24, 26, 28). God removed His protection from them and turned them over to the consequences of their evil.

Paul later refers to God's active wrath when he warned, "Because of your stubbornness and unrepentant heart you are storing up wrath for yourself in the day of wrath and revelation of the righteous judgment of God" (Romans 2:5). The Bible says, "It is a terrifying thing to fall into the hands of the living God" (Hebrew 10:31).

So God's fierce wrath against sin is as much a reflection of His character as is His love. The wrath of God is not a popular subject. I don't necessarily enjoy teaching about it. But if I didn't warn people about God's judgment, I would be like a fireman who fails to warn people about fire.

The Realm of Hell

The fourth aspect of hell I want us to see is its realm, or the physical layout of hell as best we can understand from Scripture.

The Greek word for hell that Jesus used most often is *gehenna*. When I was in Israel I saw the place that hell is named for. In Jesus' day, *gehenna* was the local garbage dump outside Jerusalem that smoldered constantly as garbage from the city was dumped there. It was also a place that constantly bred worms, which as we'll see helps add to the description of hell's horrors.

From this word alone we get the picture that hell is a wasteland completely apart from God's goodness or any factor that would moderate its horror.

The Bible also relates this terrible place to "the lake of fire and brimstone" (Revelation 20:10). Then John wrote, "Death and Hades were thrown into the lake of fire. This is the second death, the lake of fire" (v. 14).

Hades is another Greek term that was translated "hell" in the King James Version. But it is distinct from the lake of fire, the final doom of unbelievers. Hades is the place where the unrighteous go at the moment of death.

Jesus' story of the rich man and Lazarus in Luke 16 shows that Hades is a place of conscious suffering and torment. But right now it is more of a "holding cell" for unbelievers until their final judgment at the Great White Throne. That's why in Revelation 20:14, Hades as a place that holds condemned sinners is also said to be thrown into the lake of fire.

The specific mention of Hades in connection with the lake of fire suggests an arrangement in hell that I think can best be described by an illustration.

More than a mile off the coast of San Francisco is a small island on which sits Alcatraz, a former federal prison whose very name used to strike fear in the hearts of criminals.

This infamous prison was closed in 1963 and is now a tourist attraction. But in its day Alcatraz held some of the most notorious and evil criminals in America, and it was well known as a place from which successful escape was impossible.

Even if an inmate made it outside the walls, he faced a long swim in ice-cold, shark-infested water to the mainland. Several inmates who broke out of the prison disappeared and were presumed drowned trying to make it to shore.

I believe hell is constituted along something of the same lines. That is, it is a prison house for Satan and his angels and lost sinners, surrounded not by a formidable body of water but by the lake of fire.

One reason I believe that lost people in hell are in a prison house surrounded by the lake of fire, rather than in the fire itself, is because of the way the rich man in Luke 16 responded to his situation.

Jesus said, "In Hades [the rich man] lifted up his eyes, being in torment, and saw Abraham far away and Lazarus in his bosom" (Luke 16:23). Then he pleaded for relief from his suffering, and for someone to warn his brothers so they would not suffer his fate (vv. 24–31).

Notice that this man's thoughts were clear, his emotions were intact, and his mind was fully functional. The idea of hell as a place where people are out of their minds, screaming insanely with fire bursting out of them, is more of a medieval teaching than an accurate biblical understanding.

This concept of hell as a prison house surrounded by the lake of fire may raise some questions in your mind. We'll deal with these now as we change our focus a little bit and talk about the various aspects of hell.

The Physical Torment of Hell

Hell involves horrible physical torment. The rich man cried out, "Father Abraham, have mercy on me, and send Lazarus so that he may dip the tip of his finger in water and cool off my tongue, for I am in agony in this flame" (Luke 16:24).

This man was in real torment even though his body had died and was awaiting the resurrection to judgment. We know that his body wasn't yet reunited with his spirit because this won't happen for unbelievers until the resurrection at the final judgment.

We have never seen the fullness of God's wrath unleashed on sin.

According to Revelation 20:13, the sea, the grave, and Hades itself "gave up the dead which were in them" so these people could be judged and sent to hell. Just as believers will receive new bodies that will equip them for eternal life in heaven, so the lost will receive resurrected bodies that will allow them to endure eternal punishment in hell.

I would compare this to a person trapped in a burning desert with the sun beating down unmercifully twenty-four hours a day with no relief at all—not even a drop of water or an aspirin to dull the pain.

The sufferer can't just lie down and die, and there's no escape from the desert. The only choice is to keep on going and functioning every day, despite the agonizing suffering and hopelessness of the situation.

Imagine being in that environment, without one second's relief from the sun, never any water or a breeze to cool you off, and the knowledge that it will be like this forever.

And what's worse, you still have all your faculties working all the time so you can't even "tune out," or just quit thinking about it, and perhaps gain one second's worth of peace.

Make no mistake. The rich man was in immediate, intense, and unrelieved torment from the fire of God's wrath the moment he opened his eyes in hell.

We have a hard time imagining this because we have never seen the fullness of God's wrath unleashed on sin. Here on earth, His wrath is tempered by His mercy. But there is nothing to protect or insulate people in hell from the fierce, unrestrained judgment of God against sin.

The Mental Torment of Hell

The Bible teaches that the suffering of hell will also include the mental torment of memory and regret.

When the rich man of Luke 16 asked for a drop of water to cool his tongue, Abraham gave him this answer. "Child, *remember* that during your life you received your good things" (v. 25, italics added). Much of the agony of hell will be the remorse of knowing things could have been different, because people in hell will have perfect memories.

All of us know the tremendous power of regret. Some people allow themselves to be eaten up by the mental anguish of what might been if only they had or hadn't done this or that. John Greenleaf Whittier wrote that the saddest of all human words are "It might have been." In hell, every regret will be eternally remembered.

Jesus said hell is a place where "their worm does not die, and the fire is not quenched" (Mark 9:48). What did He mean by the worm that doesn't die?

This was a reference to *gehenna,* the smoldering garbage dump outside Jerusalem that became a synonym for hell. We said earlier that this place constantly bred worms because new garbage was always being dumped there. So the worms never died.

How does this apply to hell? Notice that Jesus used the pronoun "their" in identifying the worm. In other words, this worm belongs to somebody. We might call it a "personalized worm." Jesus also used the singular word *worm,* not worms.

Just as worms or maggots on earth gnaw away on a dead body until it is gone, so the worm of hell gnaws away at the life of the condemned person. But the difference is that this gnawing never stops because the life it is gnawing on is never consumed. And the gnawing is highly personalized, "their worm," because each person's level of regret will be unique to that person's life. This is the unending mental torment of hell—the churning of regret over lost opportunities for salvation, poor choices made in life, and the condemnation of others whom the lost person loved. The rich man agonized for his brothers.

I believe the mental suffering of hell will be so intense the person will be able to recall specific occasions when he or she heard the gospel of Jesus Christ and rejected it. Those times will not only be vivid, but it will seem like it all happened yesterday.

It's impossible to imagine having eternity to remember the things you would give anything to forget. When Abraham told the rich man to remember the way life was for him, nothing more needed to be said.

For Lazarus and the rich man, hell was the great reversal (Luke 16:25). This suggests another element to the mental suffering of hell. Presumably, the rich man had the same rich tastes and desires, but he would never be able to satisfy them.

Part of the suffering of hell will be the eternal desire for sin without any possibility of fulfillment. For instance, a drug addict or sex addict in hell will experience intense, burning desires for illicit drugs and illicit sex that can never be met.

Why is this so? Because the Bible indicates that when Jesus returns, not only will righteous people be confirmed in their righteousness, wicked people will be confirmed in their wickedness (see Revelation 22:11). So a morally filthy person on earth will be morally filthy for eternity in hell.

Picture an alcoholic who can't get a drink, an addict who can't get a fix, or a greedy person whose greed will never be satisfied, and you have a picture of hell.

Some people think hell will have a purifying effect on sinners, who will realize the error of their ways and become repentant. But I don't see that in the Bible. There are no nice people in hell. The angry person who could not control his anger on earth will be an eternally angry person in hell.

Hell will be the full expression of the sin nature that corrupted the human race and caused mankind to become alienated from God. The sin nature of those in hell will cry out eternally for fulfillment—only there will be none. The worm will not die.

The Spiritual Torment of Hell

I wish we could say that the physical and mental suffering of hell were the limits of its misery. But we need to talk about two more elements that are actually far worse.

We said earlier that the worst suffering in hell is the knowledge that the lost person is cut off from God forever, with no hope of forgiveness or restoration.

This part of hell's torment is heightened by the fact that according to Luke 16:23, the rich man could see Lazarus and Abraham far off in heaven. He could actually see the eternal life and joy he was missing.

Let me go back to my earlier illustration of Alcatraz prison. One of the torments of Alcatraz was that from the island, the prisoners could see the lights and the buildings of San Francisco and know they were missing out on life.

The rich man could see Lazarus in Abraham's bosom, so we can legitimately talk about what it would be like if a person in hell was able to catch glimpses of heaven. Imagine the spiritual torment of knowing you not only missed heaven, but will be eternally reminded of what you missed.

For a sufferer in hell, the torment of seeing what is being missed in heaven is one thing. But the Bible also declares that there is no fulfillment or peace of any kind in hell. "When a wicked man dies, his expectation will perish" (Proverbs 11:7). God says in Isaiah 48:22, "There is no peace for the wicked."

People in hell will not find any solace from other sufferers. All the jokes people make about wanting to go to hell to be with their friends and enjoy the parties are just so much foolishness. There will be lots of people in hell, but they won't be any company to anyone.

God says in Isaiah 66:24 that the corpses of those who rebelled against Him will "be an abhorrence to all mankind." The picture here is of defeated enemies whose bodies have been set on fire and are being eaten by worms. This is, in fact, the same phrase as Jesus used of hell in Mark 9:48.

This brings us back to the disgusting picture of *gehenna,* the garbage dump that was loathsome to see and smell. The Bible says hell will be a loathsome, degrading place. Everybody will be a stench and a disgust to everybody else.

Daniel 12:2 says the wicked will be resurrected to "disgrace and everlasting contempt." People will be contemptuous of one another in hell. How could it be otherwise when everybody's sin nature is being fully expressed?

The Eternal Torment of Hell

I want to say one more thing about hell before we turn to the joys and delights of heaven. We've said it before, but we need to emphasize again that hell is an eternal place.

In Luke 16:26, Abraham told the rich man there was "a great chasm fixed" between heaven and hell, with no possibility of bridging it. I take it that this chasm is the lake of fire that surrounds the prison house of hell, making any escape impossible.

Let me mention Revelation 14:9–11, which warns that anyone who worships the Antichrist or receives his mark will suffer eternal torment.

We don't need to belabor this point, because the Bible is crystal clear on hell's unending torment. We need to grasp the awful, eternal consequences of rejecting Christ so that we make sure we escape this place of suffering through faith in Him, and make sure that as much as it lies in our power, no one we know will have to experience God's eternal wrath on sin.

God did everything necessary to keep anyone from going to hell when He gave Jesus Christ as the substitute for the sins of the world. He has an "anti-hell" vaccine, the blood of Christ, available to all who trust Him alone for salvation and eternal life.

WHAT IS HEAVEN LIKE?

Are you ready for a change of biblical scenery? I am! Knowing the truth about hell is important, no matter how intense or difficult that truth may be. But I'm so grateful that hell isn't God's last word on eternity! Let's talk about heaven.

I'm convinced that far too many people, Christians included, think in terms of extremes rather than biblical reality when they think about heaven. One extreme is the idea that heaven is going to be a dreamy kind of existence in which we float around on clouds with nothing much to do.

Another extreme view some people take of heaven is to see it as sort of an intrusion into life on earth—something far off in the future that we don't want to happen until we have accomplished everything we wanted to do in this life.

The best way to correct both of these mistaken concepts is to see what God's Word says about heaven. God hasn't told us everything, but Scripture gives us enough glimpses and enough promises about heaven to know we don't want to miss this place of eternal joy.

I want to begin our biblical tour of heaven at a familiar place, with Jesus and His disciples in the Upper Room the night He was betrayed (John 14:1–3).

Heaven Is a Promised Place

Among the assurances Jesus gave His troubled disciples that night was this promise concerning heaven: "In My Father's house are many dwelling places; if it were not so, I would have told you; for I go to prepare a place for you" (John 14:2).

The first thing we need to know about heaven is

that it is a promised place. A promise is only as good as the integrity of the one making it and his ability to deliver on the promise. That's good news for us, because Jesus' promise of a heavenly home is based on the character of God.

Jesus had just told His disciples, "Do not let your heart be troubled; believe in God, believe also in Me" (John 14:1). In other words, we can relax because of the One making this promise.

If you ever doubt the reality of heaven, believe in the God who cannot lie. The only way heaven can be a lie is if God is a liar—and that's impossible (Numbers 23:19). This God who cannot lie has told us that when our earthly bodies collapse like an old tent, we will have new bodies that are eternal in heaven (2 Corinthians 5:1).

Jesus tied belief in God the Father with belief in Himself because He is God become flesh (John 1:14). The closer the disciples drew to Jesus, the more they came to trust Him.

We can't see Christ in the flesh today, but we can see the reality of His work in our lives. And the more real Jesus becomes to us, the more we come to trust in Him.

The promise of heaven rests on another firm pillar, the inerrant Word of the God we can trust not to lie to us.

The Bible says our citizenship is in heaven (Philippians 3:20). It's where we really belong. We're just aliens passing through down here. According to 1 Peter 1:4, we have an inheritance reserved for us in heaven.

When you make a reservation at a hotel, you don't need to see the hotel ahead of time to know the reservation is firm. You are given a confirmation number, and based on the integrity of the hotel's name and reputation, you take it by faith that a real hotel in a real city will have a room for you when you arrive.

Our reservation in heaven is secure, written in the blood of Jesus Christ. We have His Word on it!

Since our citizenship and inheritance as believers are in heaven, it makes sense that heaven is where we should store our treasures. Jesus said, "Store up for yourselves treasures in heaven" (Matthew 6:20). That would be misleading advice if heaven were not real.

God's Word says our total identity and worth as Christians are linked to heaven, a promised place. This is why we can be passionate about heaven, like the early believers were.

The writer of Hebrews says the saints of old received and believed God's promises, and went about as "strangers and exiles on the earth" because they desired "a better country, that is, a heavenly one" (Hebrews 11:13, 16). Their hopes were set on heaven, not on earth. And they were not disappointed.

Heaven Is a Particular Place

Here's another feature or characteristic of heaven. By *particular* I mean heaven isn't some nebulous, indistinct concept floating out there in the universe.

Back in John 14, Jesus called heaven "My Father's house" (v. 2). God is not a nebulous concept, but a distinct Person. His house, or heaven, isn't fuzzy either. This place has an address. It's a particular location.

In fact, heaven is such a particular place that the Bible specifically calls it "the third heaven" (2 Corinthians 12:2). That distinguishes heaven from the other two heavens in the universe, the atmospheric heavens and outer space, the region of the planets and stars.

The third heaven is the dwelling place of God and the future home of believers. We know this is a particular place because when Jesus rose from the dead and ascended, He went back to heaven to sit at the right hand of God (Hebrews 1:3).

Jesus said He was returning to His Father (John 16:10). If I tell you I am going to Los Angeles, you assume I am going to a particular place because there is a city called Los Angeles. It's the same with Jesus returning to heaven. He returned to a place where He sits today at the right hand of His Father.

God also helps us understand that heaven is a particular place by showing us its capital—what we might call "downtown heaven." One reason the Bible describes the "new Jerusalem" in Revelation 21:1–22:5 is so that from this one city, we can get an idea of what the rest of heaven is like.

The apostle John wrote,

> [An angel] carried me away in the Spirit to a great and high mountain, and showed me the holy city, Jerusalem, coming down out of heaven from God, having the glory of God. Her brilliance was like a very costly stone, as a stone of crystal-clear jasper. (Revelation 21:10–11)

John went on to describe this awesome city that is fifteen hundred miles in each direction (v. 16). We will deal with the indescribable beauty of the new Jerusalem later, so I just want to note it here. It's no wonder Paul said that when he was taken to heaven and given a vision of God's dwelling place, he saw things he was not permitted to talk about.

Don't let anyone tell you that heaven is just a "pie in the sky, by and by" mystical concept. It's a particular place. Those who know Christ aren't going to "never-never land" when they die.

Heaven Is a Paternal Place

I love this characteristic of heaven. It's a family affair, a gathering of a Father with His children. Jesus called it the *"Father's* house" (John 14:2, italics added).

We need to know some important things about our heavenly Father's house. First, there is plenty of room for everybody because this house has "many dwelling places" (v. 2), what we might call apartments. The Father has made room for all of us.

But since heaven is God the Father's house, only those who are His children will live there. If God is not your Father through faith in Jesus Christ, you don't get to move into this house.

Another important fact about this house is that it reflects the nature and character of the Father who is building it and who owns it.

I have a wonderful father whom I love dearly. He and Mom still live in the same old house in inner-city

Baltimore where they raised their four children. Dad never wanted to move because this was home.

Given the age of the house and the community in which it is located, my father has made his house into the best possible place it could be. It reflects his character.

If you go to visit Arthur Evans, you will have no doubt that this home is my father's house. The rules are still in place. Even today, when my family goes to Baltimore, we are going to Daddy's house.

But my earthly father is limited in power and in knowledge, and he's limited to time and space. My heavenly Father suffers from none of these limitations, and when I'm with Him in His house I'll enjoy unlimited fellowship, full knowledge, and other things that it isn't possible to enjoy here on earth.

It's important for us to realize that heaven is the Father's house because the better we get to know our Father now, the better we will be able to understand and appreciate heaven.

That's because heaven is consumed with the Person and the worship of God. Revelation 21:23 says heaven "has no need of the sun or of the moon to shine on it, for the glory of God has illumined it, and its lamp is the Lamb."

Heaven is where God fully expresses Himself. We will know Him without being hindered by our sin or being hampered by the fact that God works through other agencies as He does here on earth.

For example, God uses the sun and moon to light the earth. But it's not that way in heaven. There the glory of God comes out from under the wraps and shines in its fullness. Heaven doesn't need any sun because God's glory lights the place up all the time. And His light will never go out, so there's no night in heaven (Revelation 21:25).

Heaven is the Father's place because it is permeated by His presence and His glory. His children will bask in the undiminished fullness of the Father. It will be staggering.

Heaven Is a Populated Place

Just in case you are worried about being a little lonely in heaven, let me show you some of the crowd that is going to share heaven with you. Hebrews 12:22–23 says, "You have come to Mount Zion and to the city of the living God, the heavenly Jerusalem, and to myriads of angels, to the general assembly and church of the firstborn who are enrolled in heaven, and to God, the Judge of all, and to the spirits of the righteous made perfect."

First, the heavenly city will be populated by countless millions of angels. Angels you can't see surround God's people right now. But you will be able to see them in heaven, because you will have a spiritual body.

The writer of Hebrews also said the church of Jesus Christ will be in heaven, all those who have put their trust in Christ for salvation. So your spiritual family will be there.

One of our church members asked me if we will know each other once we get to heaven. The answer is that we won't really know each other *until* we get to heaven. Why? Because we cannot fully know each other now. All I can know about other people is what I see and what they tell me. And that's not all there is to a person. But in heaven all the masks and the pretense will be removed, and we will know each other as God created us to be.

Another group of people in heaven is the Old Testament saints, called "the spirits of the righteous made perfect" (Hebrews 12:23).

You'll be able to go down to the corner of Gold Street and Silver Boulevard, run into Abraham, and ask him a few questions. David can tell you the story of how he killed Goliath. You can ask Jonah what it felt like to be swallowed by a fish and live inside of it for three days.

You'll be in heaven with all of these people because heaven is a populated place. God created it to be inhabited. John said he saw in heaven "a great multitude which no one could count" (Revelation 7:9).

Heaven Is a Prepared Place

The picture the Bible gives us of heaven just keeps getting better and better. Jesus told His disciples that He was preparing heaven for them.

Whenever we go back home to Baltimore, my mother always makes everything ready. She goes shopping so we have plenty of food in the house, and she gets the rooms ready. Everything is prepared in anticipation of my family's arrival.

That's the good news about the preparations Jesus is making in heaven. Your place in heaven is being prepared with *you* in mind.

Although heaven will be filled with people, it will also be personalized for each believer. In fact, we will help determine how well our dwelling place in heaven is decorated by the number of spiritual rewards we send on ahead of our arrival.

The story is told of a very rich woman who went to heaven, only to find out that her gardener had a bigger house than she did. She wasn't too happy about it, so she asked how that could be. The answer was, "We just used the material you sent up."

We know from passages like 1 Corinthians 3:10–15 that although all believers make it to heaven equally, the rewards they receive are not equal. Some will have gold, silver, and precious stones to present to Christ, while others will only have wood, hay, and straw, which will be burned up.

If you want an idea of what it means for God to prepare heaven with us in mind, look at Adam and Eve in the Garden of Eden. God tailor-made this paradise for them, providing everything they could possibly need or want. He even made provision for direct fellowship with Himself. No detail was overlooked.

Eden was spoiled by sin, but at the end of this age God is going to melt down the current creation (2 Peter 3:10) and replace it with new heavens and a new earth. That's part of the preparation He is making for us in heaven.

The result of this retooling is that the rest of creation will look like the new Jerusalem of Revelation 21. So as you travel around the universe in eternity, you will be dazzled by God's elaborate preparations wherever you go. God is preparing a place of unimaginable beauty for us.

Heaven Is a Personal Place

Here's another aspect of heaven that will be glorious. It's a personal place because Jesus wants us to be there with Him. "I will come again and receive you to Myself, that where I am, there you may be also" (John 14:3).

Before we get too excited about heaven, Jesus wants us to get excited about being with Him first. Being with Jesus in face-to-face fellowship for all eternity is what will make heaven so heavenly.

All the beauty of heaven is really just the backdrop, the scenery, for your eternal relationship with Christ. The central thing of heaven is that we will see our Savior face-to-face and be with Him for eternity.

I have a new appreciation for the personal side of heaven after going to Hawaii with my wife, Lois, for a preaching engagement and some time together.

The natural beauty of Hawaii is spectacular. The water was beautiful, and the weather was perfect—not too hot or too cool. Even when it rained, it was like a mist falling through the sunshine. A real paradise.

But as beautiful as Hawaii was, if Lois had not been able to go with me, I would not have gone because I didn't want to be there alone. The joy of being in a paradise is to enjoy it with somebody you love.

What made Hawaii special for me was not just walking on the beach, but walking the beach hand-in-hand with Lois and talking with her on the patio. What made the trip special was that I shared it with the most important person on earth to me. The beauty was just the backdrop for the pursuit of our love relationship.

Brother, do you remember when you were dating the woman who would become your wife? When you took her to a restaurant, you weren't just concerned about the quality of the food. You wanted to know what kind of ambiance the restaurant had, because you wanted everything to be just right while you were sitting there telling this girl how special she was and how much you loved her. You wanted candlelight and soft music and flowers and waiters in black coats with little towels over their arms coming to serve you.

That's what God is doing in heaven. He's preparing a place where you and your Savior can be together forever.

Heaven Is a Place of Perfect Beauty

Are you getting the idea that heaven is going to be a wonderful place? It's not only personally prepared by God for us, it is also a place of infinite perfections.

It's interesting that when the apostle John saw the vision of the new Jerusalem coming down from God, he described the city as "a bride adorned for her husband" (Revelation 21:2).

That's a great analogy, because when a bride comes down the aisle on her wedding day, everyone stands and looks at her in awe. She has gone through great detail in preparing for her wedding, and she is flawless in her beauty.

That's how the apostle John saw the new Jerusalem. When this "capital city" of heaven comes down from God, we are going to gasp in amazement at its beauty. We won't have words to express what we are seeing. It will literally take our breath away.

We noted earlier that this is a huge city. According to Revelation 21:16, the new Jerusalem is as tall as it is wide, fifteen hundred miles in each direction.

Fifteen hundred miles is the distance from the Atlantic coast of the United States westward to the Rockies, about half of the U.S. Imagine a city reaching out that far, and then imagine the same city reaching up to that same height. This is a high-rise unlike anything you have ever seen before, with believers occupying apartments in every tier.

Everywhere you go in heaven you will be totally surrounded by God's glory!

The city has twelve gates emblazoned with the names of the twelve tribes of Israel, and twelve foundation stones emblazoned with the names of the twelve apostles (vv. 12–14). These represent all the Old Testament and New Testament saints.

John went on to say that the entire city is pure gold, the foundation stones of the wall are adorned with every kind of precious stone, each of the twelve gates is a single pearl, and the street is pure gold (vv. 18–21).

But that's not all. These are transparent jewels. Look at Revelation 21:18, where John wrote, "The material of the wall was jasper; and the city was pure gold, like clear glass." In verse 11, John said the new Jerusalem is like "a stone of crystal-clear jasper."

There is no such thing as transparent gold on earth. But the perfect beauty of heaven includes a city made of gold and precious stones you can actually see through.

I don't think our minds can fully grasp a high-rise city half as wide as the United States, and as tall as it is wide—all made of transparent gold and jewels!

The beauty we will behold in heaven is unimaginable. And we will be able to behold it all the time, since the lights will never go out in heaven (Revelation 21:23; 22:5).

But since we're trying to imagine the unimaginable, think about what heaven must look like with the undiminished glory of God continuously illuminating all the tiers of this crystal-clear, transparent city. His glory will be reflected and refracted off every corner of the new Jerusalem.

In other words, everywhere you go in heaven you will be totally surrounded by God's glory!

Heaven Is a Place of Perfect Worship

Heaven is every preacher's dream because it is a place of perfect worship.

During his vision of heaven John wrote, "I heard a loud voice from the throne, saying, 'Behold, the tabernacle of God is among men, and He will dwell among them, and they shall be His people, and God Himself will be among them'" (Revelation 21:3).

The tabernacle in the Old Testament served largely the same purpose as the church building does today. It was the place where people went to worship God.

One reason we need to go to church is to be reminded of God. Satan tries to make us forget God the minute we walk out of the church on Sunday, and all week long we are engaged in a spiritual battle with an enemy who wants to blot God from our memory.

But in heaven there will be no tabernacle or temple (Revelation 21:22), no place we need to go to be reminded of God. It's not necessary, because in heaven we will be surrounded by and engulfed in His presence.

I can hear someone saying, "You mean heaven is like being in church all day long every day?" I know some people feel that way when Sunday morning comes around. "It's Sunday. Gotta go to church again."

But anyone who feels that way doesn't understand worship. Worship was never meant to be an exercise held in a building once a week. Paul stated the essence of worship when he said, "Whether, then, you eat or drink or whatever you do, do all to the glory of God"

(1 Corinthians 10:31). True worship is every area of our lives reflecting the true glory of God.

So the issue isn't whether you are in church all day in heaven. It's that everything you are and do throughout eternity will reflect who and what God is and bring Him eternal glory.

Since heaven itself is God's temple, every place we go, everything we do, and every conversation we have will be an act of worship. This is worship as it was meant to be.

We will live in God's reflected glory all the time, and there will never be a moment when His presence doesn't affect us. We will never feel distant from God or alone or cut off from Him. Heaven will be pure, eternal worship.

Heaven Is a Place of Perfect Pleasure

I don't think there is a Christian who has ever lived who has read Revelation 21:4 without longing for the day when God "will wipe away every tear from their eyes; and there will no longer be any death; there will no longer be any mourning, or crying, or pain; the first things have passed away."

All of the things that make life on earth hard will be wiped away in heaven. We are talking about a place of perfect, righteous pleasure.

This is possible because God says, "I am making all things new" (v. 5). So whatever we have in heaven, it will never grow old. The newness will never wear off. We will never get bored with the old stuff we have and long for new stuff.

You've heard people get up in the morning and say, "I feel like a new person today." They're expressing the joy of feeling good that particular day. In heaven, that feeling will be an ongoing reality. We will always feel like new people! There will be no pain or death because we will never grow old.

You'll also never have any reason to cry in heaven. Psalm 16:11 says that in the Lord's presence we will experience full joy.

Why aren't we experiencing this fullness of joy and righteous pleasure here on earth? After all, James says, "Every good thing given and every perfect gift is from above, coming down from the Father of lights, with whom there is no variation or shifting shadow" (James 1:17).

Everything good we have in life comes from the hand of God, whether it's health or family or material blessings. The reason we don't always enjoy these things is not because of God, but because of what James calls the "shifting shadow."

This refers to the ups and downs, the ebbs and flows of life. People can cause a shadow to come across our lives. Our own sin often plunges us into darkness. The devil seeks to cause shifting shadows to interrupt life. All of us shift and move while God, like the sun at the center of the solar system, remains the same.

So one moment I'm in the sunlight of God, and I'm smiling. But the next moment I'm crying because life has cast a dark shadow across my path. My circumstances have shifted.

But heaven doesn't have any shadows because there is nothing to create a shadow. Heaven is perfect daylight and perfect joy all the time because God is the Light of heaven.

Heaven Is a Place of Perfect Knowledge

Heaven will also be marked by perfect knowledge of God. The fog surrounding our minds down here will disappear.

I like the way Paul described this in 1 Corinthians 13:12. "For now we see in a mirror dimly, but then face to face; now I know in part, but then I will know fully just as I also have been fully known."

When we are in heaven there will no breaks in our system of knowledge. There will be nothing we cannot discover with our minds, because our capacity to receive God's truth will be so much different. The secrets of God will be unveiled, and we will know as we are known.

There will never be an end to our learning in heaven, nothing to block or hinder our knowledge. We will never forget what we learn. That ought to be good news to you if you're the kind of learner who has trouble retaining information!

Our knowledge will be perfect in heaven because we will see God face-to-face (Revelation 22:4). In other words, nothing will come between us and God to cloud our vision of Him.

When I was growing up, if I needed to know something I had to go to the encyclopedia or use flash cards.

Not today. Now I connect my computer to the Internet, and a world of knowledge is literally at my fingertips. If mankind can do this, think what heaven will be like in terms of access to information. And all the data we receive will be perfect truth.

Heaven Is a Place of Perfect Life

One reason we know that heaven is a place of perfect life is that there will be no pain or sorrow or death there. Perfect life certainly demands the absence of death.

Heaven's perfect life is also described in Revelation 22:1–2, where we see "a river of the water of life" and "the tree of life."

Heaven is a place of perfect life because we will have perfect, glorified spiritual bodies made like Jesus' glorified body (Philippians 3:21). According to 1 John 3:2, when we see Christ we will be like Him.

This tells us what our bodies are going to be like in heaven. Christ did some remarkable things after He rose from the dead, including traveling anywhere at will despite closed doors or any other obstacle. In our glorified bodies we will have the ability to transport ourselves from one dimension to another simply by deciding to do it.

But there is one thing a spiritual body will no longer be able to do, and won't need to do, and that is engage in physical relationships like those we experienced on earth.

That's why Jesus said in heaven we will be like the

angels, who do not marry (Mark 12:25). There will be no need for procreation in heaven. The unending delight of God's presence will completely overshadow any experience or relationship we could have down here.

People often ask if we will recognize each other in heaven. Absolutely! Mary recognized Jesus on resurrection morning (John 20:16). The multitude John saw in heaven included people from every tribe and nationality on earth (Revelation 7:9), which tells me that we will retain our racial and ethnic identities, as well as our personal identities, in heaven.

Before we leave this section, I want to look at an interesting concept with you. It has to do with the statement in Revelation 22:2 that the leaves of the tree of life are for "the healing of the nations."

Didn't we just read that there is no death or pain in heaven? If heaven is a perfect place and we have resurrected, glorified spiritual bodies, why do we need a tree that produces healing? Why the need for a tree that produces life when we already have eternal life?

A possible answer lies in Revelation 21:24–26, in the description of the new Jerusalem. "The nations will walk by its light, and the kings of the earth will bring their glory into it. . . . Its gates will never be closed; and they will bring the glory and the honor of the nations into it."

John is talking about a group of people who have access to the heavenly Jerusalem, but don't live there. He says kings and others come and go from the city, bringing their glory into it.

In order to have kings, there have to be kingdoms for them to rule. John says there are people living outside the new Jerusalem who visit the city and bring their homage to God, the way pilgrims in our day might visit Mecca. Who are these people, and why do they need the healing leaves of the tree of life?

There is only one group of people left on earth to go into eternity in their physical bodies—those who were true to Jesus Christ and served Him during His millennial kingdom. They go into eternity after the Millennium with *physical* glorified bodies, not spiritual glorified bodies like we will have, because they did not experience death and resurrection.

We will have perfect, productive, eternally fulfilling service to perform.

To put in another way, these people will go into eternity with bodies like Adam and Eve had at their creation before they were flawed by sin. Their perfect physical bodies will be maintained through a special provision from God.

The Bible indicates that the new, renovated earth will be occupied in eternity. This group from the Millennium will fill the earth because they will still be able to procreate. These people will make up the nations who

48

do not live in the new Jerusalem, but will have access to the city.

Why? To pay homage to God and bring Him their worship, and because they will need the leaves of the tree of life for their continued health and well-being. These people will carry on life as we know it, except without sin, as they fill the earth.

So heaven will be a place of perfect life, even for those who do not get to live and reign with Christ in the new Jerusalem. The saints will be the privileged ones, sharing the glories of heaven with the Lord continually.

Heaven Is a Place of Perfect Service

The last thing I want to discuss about heaven certainly isn't the least in importance. It helps to answer the question of what we will be doing in heaven for all eternity.

As he described the joys of the new Jerusalem, John said, "The throne of God and of the Lamb will be in it, and His bond-servants will serve Him" (Revelation 22:3). That's you and me. We were saved to serve God here on earth, and we will continue serving Him in heaven.

The concept of people living on the new earth in physical bodies, and having access to the new Jerusalem to worship God, suggests that heaven will be filled with organizations and structures that need management.

So don't worry about being bored in eternity. We are going to be serving God as His bond-servants, managing the universe. We will have perfect, productive, eternally fulfilling service to perform.

Revelation 5:10 indicates that part of our service will be spiritual or religious in nature, in that God will make us "to be a kingdom and priests to our God." Jesus' parable in Luke 19 suggests that His faithful servants on earth will be put in charge of "cities" in heaven (vv. 17, 19), so we will also have various levels of administrative responsibilities.

I heard of one man who said all he wanted to do in heaven was sit in his lawn chair and drink iced tea. We mentioned earlier that a lot of people have the erroneous idea that heaven will be some sort of dreamy, floating existence in the clouds.

But that's not what the Bible says. We are going to be busy working for the Lord. Many people like to believe that work is a result of the curse. But Adam was given charge of the Garden of Eden to manage it before the fall into sin (Genesis 2:15).

That means God-glorifying, personally fulfilling work is part of His original plan for creation. It was only after Adam sinned that his work caused him to sweat. Like everything else marred by sin, work needs to be redeemed, not abolished.

A lot of people don't want to go to work every day either because they don't like their jobs, they are bored with what they're doing, or the job doesn't pay enough.

But heaven doesn't have any of these problems. You will never get tired, and you will be totally fulfilled every time you do anything. Serving God as His priests and administrators will be the most rewarding thing we have ever done.

A Down Payment on Heaven

If you're like me, the more you talk about heaven the more you wish you could experience some of heaven right now.

Well, you can. God has given us the Holy Spirit as the "pledge" or down payment on our redemption (Ephesians 1:13–14). The Spirit's presence in our lives is God's assurance that someday He will complete our salvation by taking us to heaven.

But in the meantime, it's the Holy Spirit's job to give us a taste of heaven today. The Spirit wants to lift our spirits to the third heaven so we can have a heavenly experience even while we're on earth.

I like to compare our anticipation of heaven to the story of Cinderella. She had to live with a wicked stepmother and wicked stepsisters, but when she went to the ball she met a prince. And even though she had to go back to her hard existence for a while, her life was never the same because her prince didn't forget her. He came one day and took her away to his castle to be his bride.

Right now you and I have to live with a wicked stepmother called the devil and wicked stepsisters called demons. Sometimes our lives can be hard because we are living under the curse of sin.

But God wants you to remember that even while you are ironing clothes and scrubbing floors, the Prince named Jesus Christ is coming back to get you someday and take you to be with Him forever. That's heaven, and it's going to be glorious.

THE URBAN ALTERNATIVE

The Philosophy

Dr. Tony Evans and TUA believe the answer to transforming our culture comes from the inside out and from the bottom up. We believe the core cause of the problems we face is a spiritual one; therefore, the only way to address them is spiritually. And that means the proclamation and application of biblical principles to the four areas of life—the individual, the family, the church, and the community. We've tried a political, social, economic, and even a religious agenda. It's time for a kingdom agenda.

The Purpose

We believe that when each biblical sphere of life functions properly, the net result is evangelism, discipleship, and community impact. As people learn how to govern themselves under God, they then transform the institutions of family, church, and government from a biblically based kingdom perspective.

The Programs

To achieve our goal we use a variety of strategies, methods, and resources for reaching and equipping as many people as possible.

- Broadcast Media

  The Urban Alternative reaches hundreds of thousands of people each day with a kingdom-based approach to life through its daily radio program, weekly television broadcast, and the Internet.

- Leadership Training

  Our national Church Development Conference, held annually, equips pastors and lay leaders to become agents of change. Teaching biblical methods of church ministry has helped congregations renew their sense of mission and expand their ministry impact.

- Crusades/Conferences

  Crusades are designed to bring churches together across racial, cultural, and denominational lines to win the lost. TUA also seeks to keep these churches together for ongoing fellowship and community impact. Conferences give Christians practical biblical insight on how to live victoriously in accordance with God's Word and His kingdom agenda in the four areas of life—personal, family, church, and community.

- Resource Development

  We are fostering lifelong learning partnerships with the people we serve by providing a variety of published materials. We offer books, audiotapes, videos, and booklets to strengthen people in their walk with God and ministry to others.

- **Project Turn-Around**
  PTA is a comprehensive church-based community impact strategy. It addresses such areas as economic development, education, housing, health revitalization, family renewal and reconciliation. To model the success of the project, TUA invests in its own program locally. We also assist other churches in tailoring the model to meet the specific needs of their communities, while simultaneously addressing the spiritual and moral frame of reference.

* * *

For more information, a catalog of Dr. Tony Evans's ministry resources, and a complimentary copy of Dr. Evans's monthly devotional magazine,
call (800) 800-3222 or
write TUA at P.O. Box 4000, Dallas TX 75208.